ANIM

by Michèle Dufresne • Illustrated by Sterling Lamet

Pioneer Valley Educational Press, Inc.

"Here is my dog," said Tony.
"My dog can do tricks!
Can Jasper do tricks?"

"Oh, yes," said Katie.
"Jasper can do tricks."

"My dog can shake hands,"
said Tony.
"Look at my dog
shaking hands."

Tony looked at Jasper.
"Can Jasper shake hands?"
he said.

"No," said Katie.

"My dog can beg,"
said Tony.
"Look at my dog begging."

Tony looked at Jasper.
"Can Jasper beg?" he said.

"No," said Katie.

"Look," said Tony.
"My dog can roll over.
Look at my dog
rolling over!"

Tony looked at Jasper.
"Can Jasper roll over?"
he said.

"No," said Katie.

"My cat can read,"
said Katie.
"Jasper, where is
the tuna fish?"

"Look at Jasper reading!"